FINGERPICKING
EARLY JAZZ STANDARDS

Arrangements by Steve Howell
For more information on Steve Howell visit **www.stevehowell.ws**

ISBN 978-1-5400-2723-8

Visit Hal Leonard Online at
www.halleonard.com

World headquarters, contact:
Hal Leonard
7777 West Bluemound Road
Milwaukee, WI 53213
Email: info@halleonard.com

In Europe, contact:
Hal Leonard Europe Limited
1 Red Place
London, W1K 6PL
Email: info@halleonardeurope.com

In Australia, contact:
Hal Leonard Australia Pty. Ltd.
4 Lentara Court
Cheltenham, Victoria, 3192 Australia
Email: info@halleonard.com.au

INTRODUCTION TO FINGERSTYLE GUITAR

Fingerstyle (a.k.a. fingerpicking) is a guitar technique that means you literally pick the strings with your right-hand fingers and thumb. This contrasts with the conventional technique of strumming and playing single notes with a pick (a.k.a. flatpicking). For fingerpicking, you can use any type of guitar: acoustic steel-string, nylon-string classical, or electric.

THE RIGHT HAND

The most common right-hand position is shown here.

Use a high wrist; arch your palm as if you were holding a ping-pong ball. Keep the thumb outside and away from the fingers, and let the fingers do the work rather than lifting your whole hand.

The thumb generally plucks the bottom strings with downstrokes on the left side of the thumb and thumbnail. The other fingers pluck the higher strings using upstrokes with the fleshy tip of the fingers and fingernails. The thumb and fingers should pluck one string per stroke and not brush over several strings.

Another picking option you may choose to use is called hybrid picking (a.k.a. plectrum-style fingerpicking). Here, the pick is usually held between the thumb and first finger, and the three remaining fingers are assigned to pluck the higher strings.

THE LEFT HAND

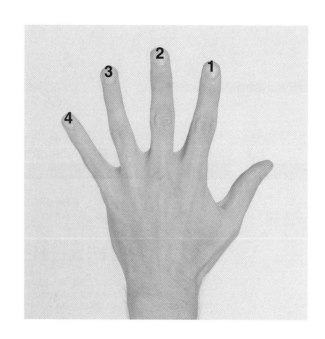

The left-hand fingers are numbered 1 through 4.

Be sure to keep your fingers arched, with each joint bent; if they flatten out across the strings, they will deaden the sound when you fingerpick. As a general rule, let the strings ring as long as possible when playing fingerstyle.

Blue Skies
from BETSY
Words and Music by Irving Berlin

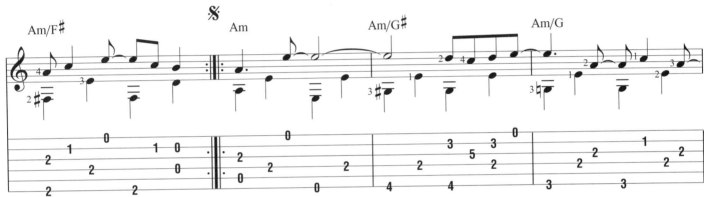

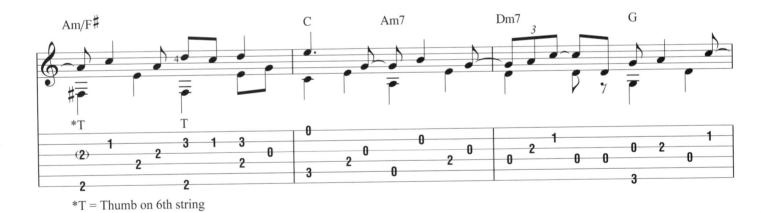

*T = Thumb on 6th string

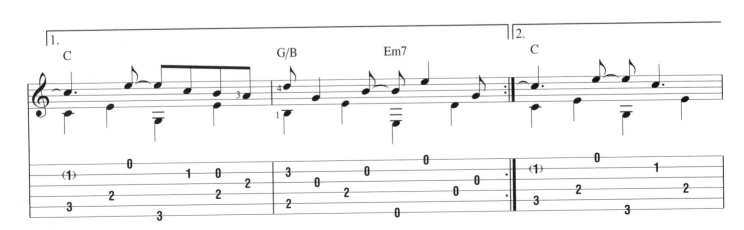

But Not for Me
from GIRL CRAZY
Music and Lyrics by George Gershwin and Ira Gershwin

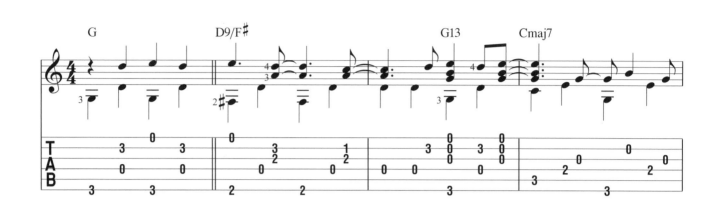

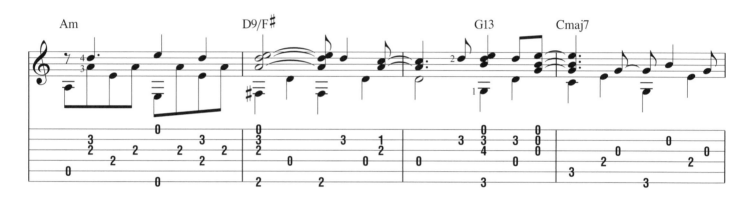

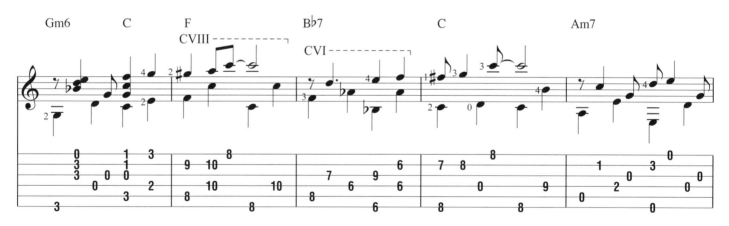

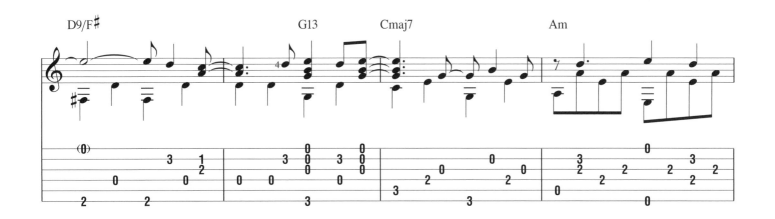

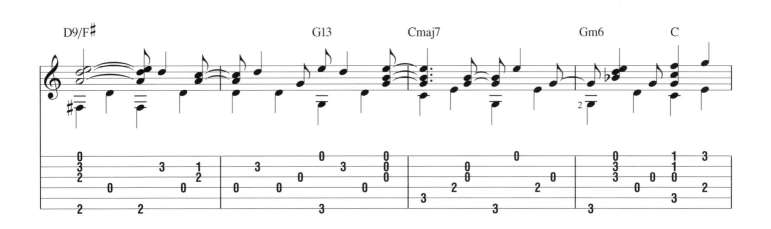

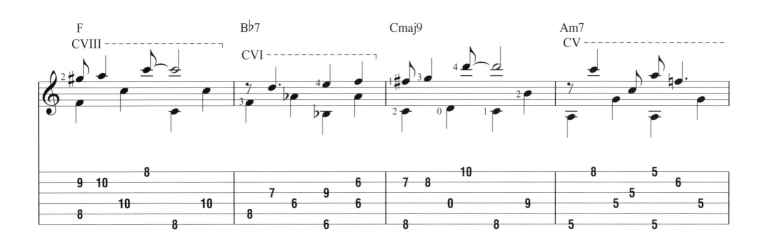

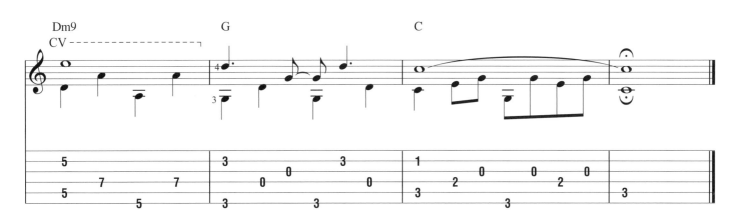

Bye Bye Blackbird

from PETE KELLY'S BLUES

Words by Mort Dixon
Music by Ray Henderson

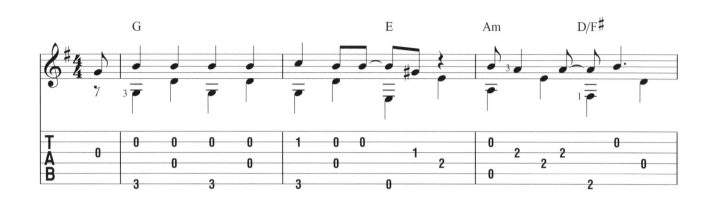

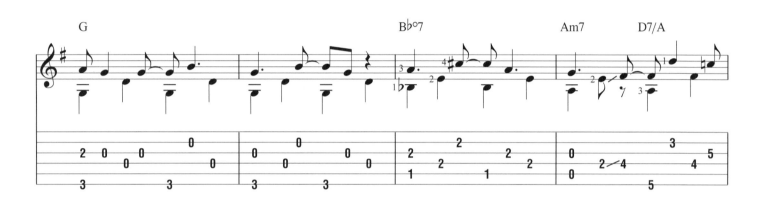

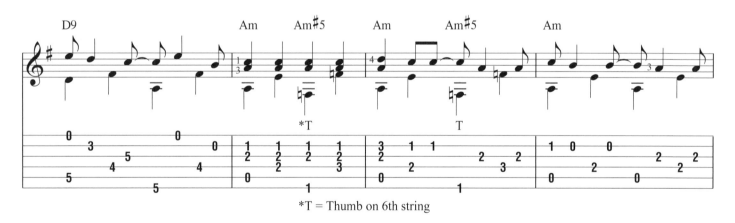

*T = Thumb on 6th string

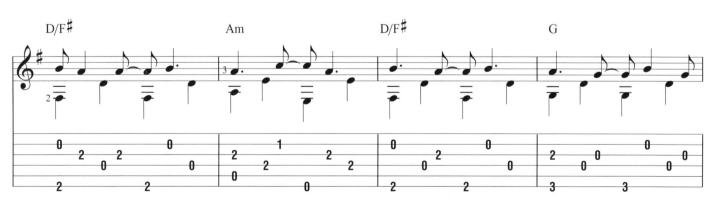

I'll See You in My Dreams

Words by Gus Kahn
Music by Isham Jones

*3rd finger   **As before

Lover, Come Back to Me

from THE NEW MOON

Lyrics by Oscar Hammerstein II
Music by Sigmund Romberg

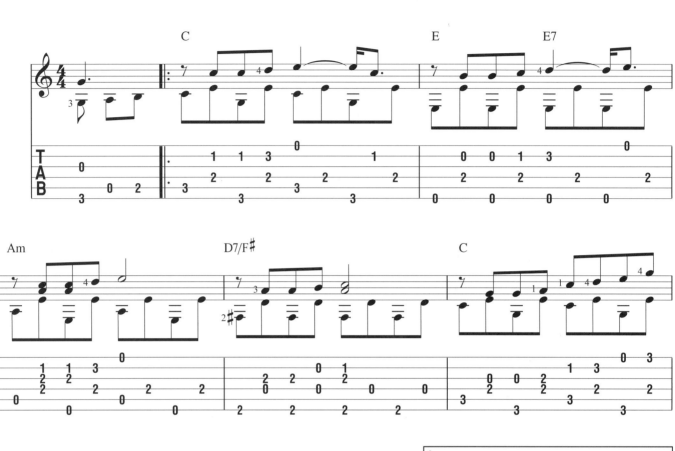

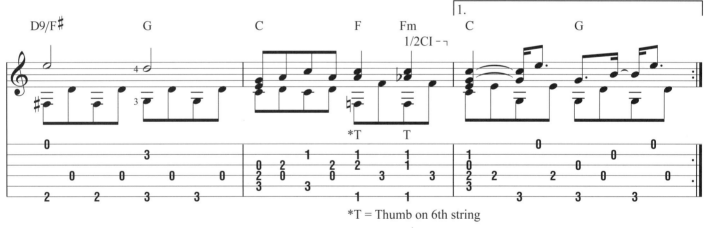

*T = Thumb on 6th string

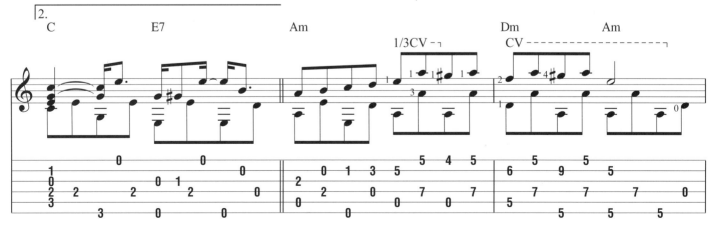

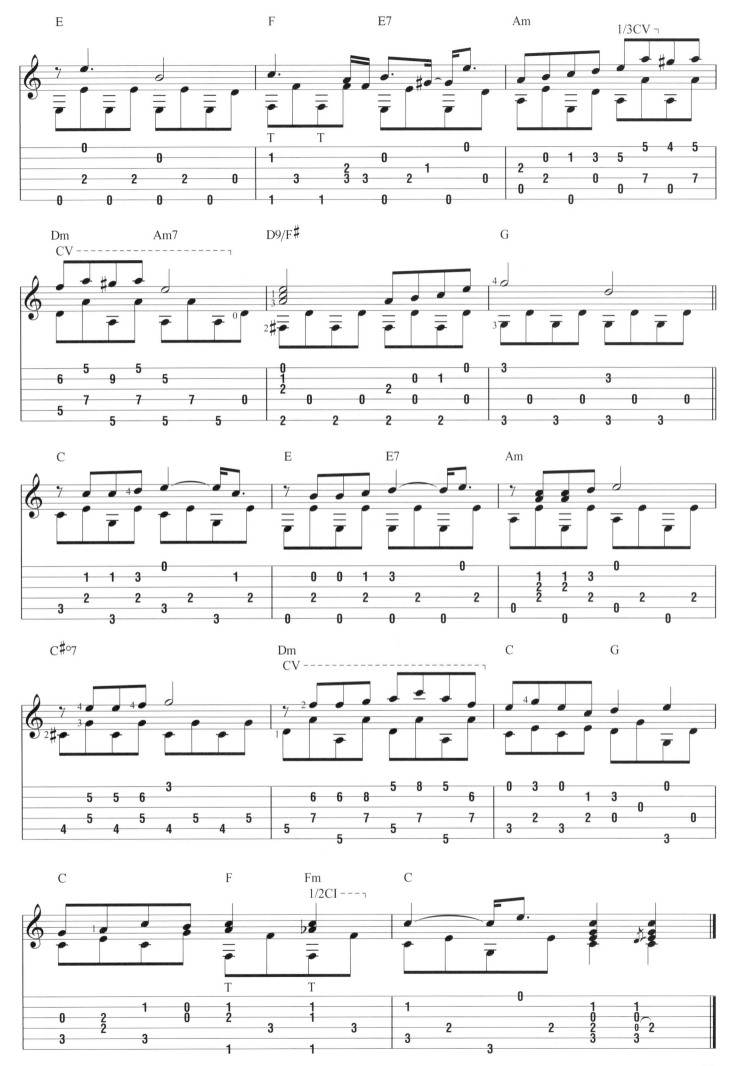

Mood Indigo

Words and Music by Duke Ellington, Irving Mills and Albany Bigard

*T = Thumb on 6th string

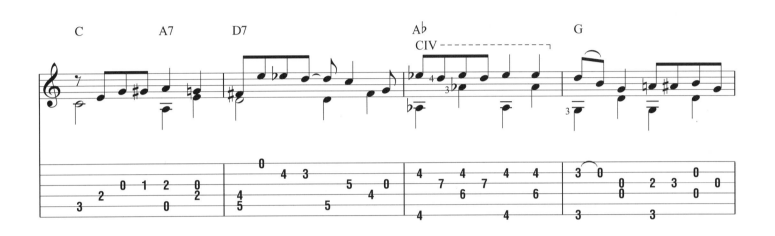

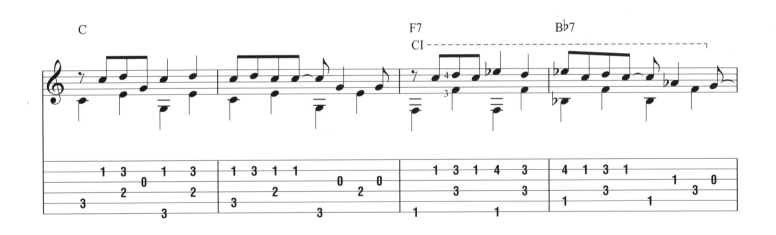

Muskrat Ramble

Written by Edward Ory

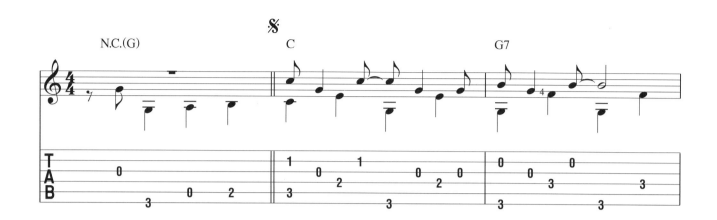

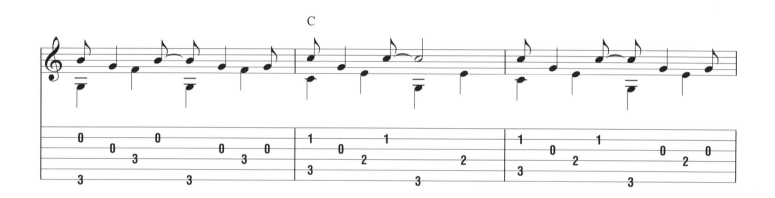

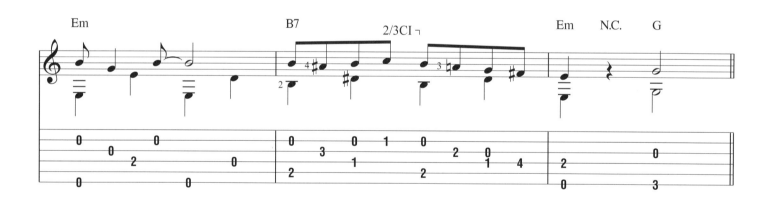

St. Louis Blues
from BIRTH OF THE BLUES
Words and Music by W.C. Handy

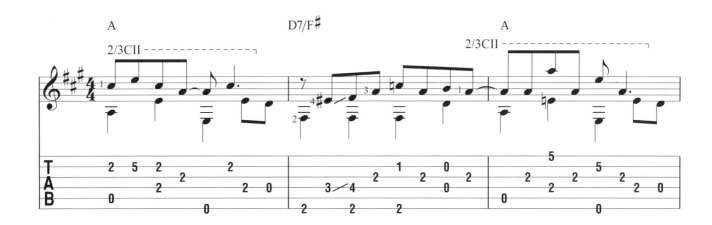

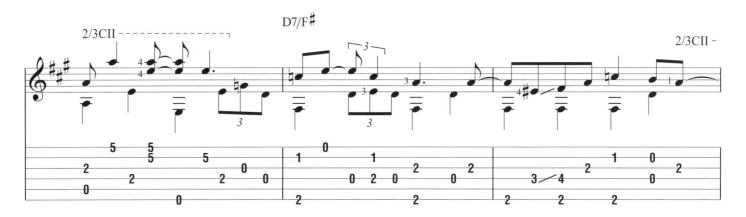

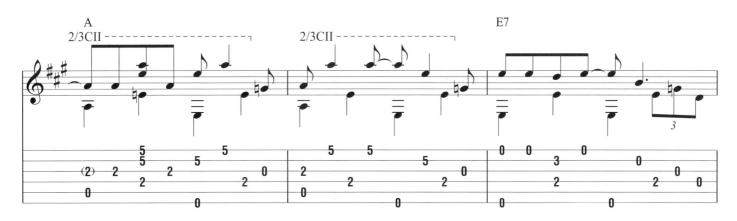

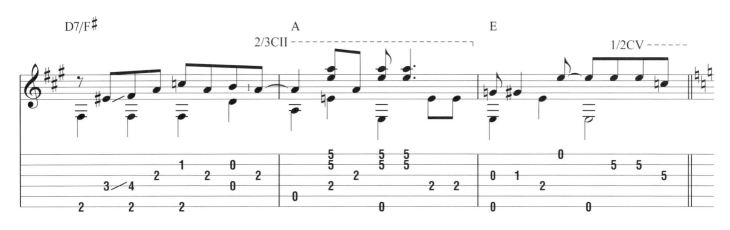

20

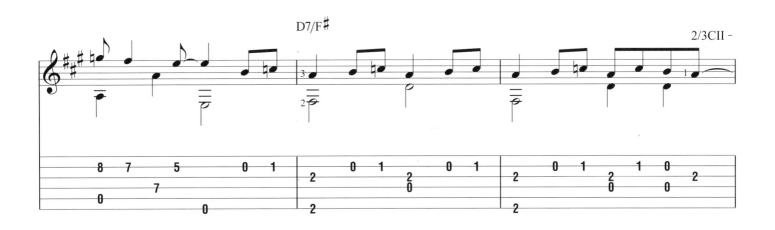

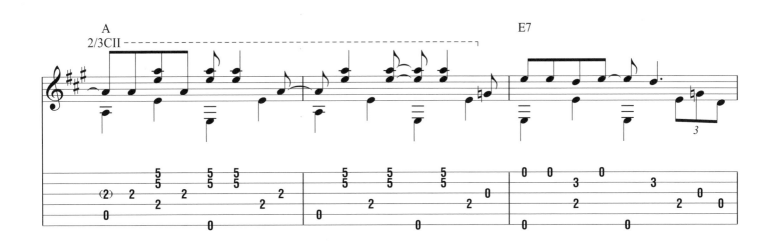

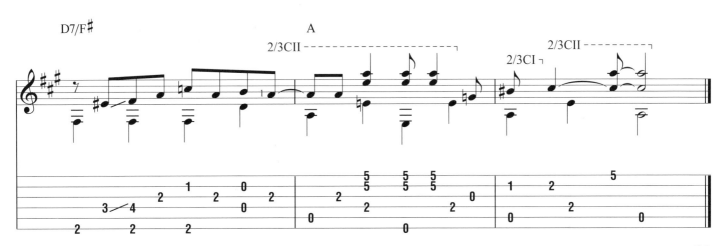

My Melancholy Baby

Words by George Norton
Music by Ernie Burnett

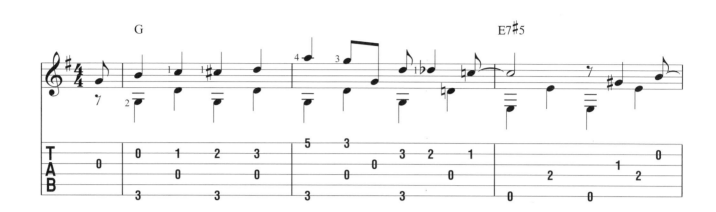

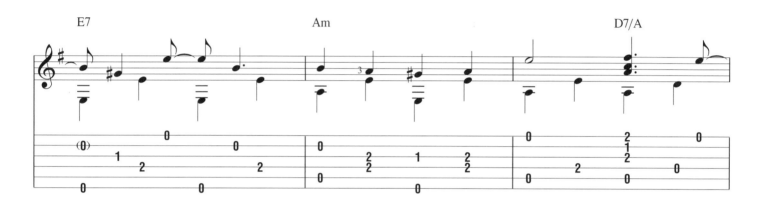

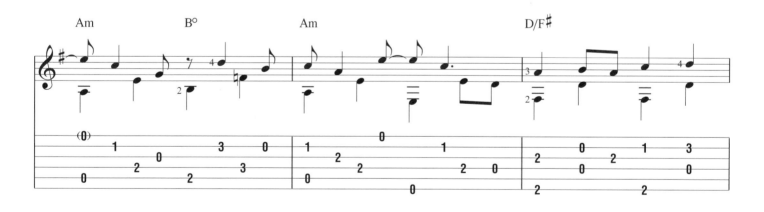

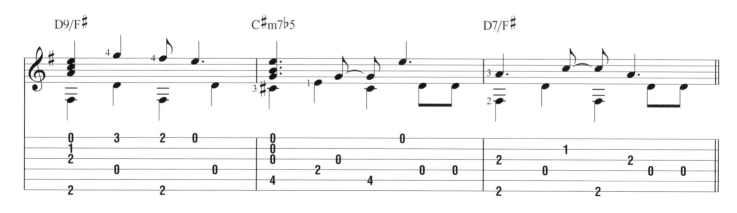

23

On the Sunny Side of the Street

Lyric by Dorothy Fields
Music by Jimmy McHugh

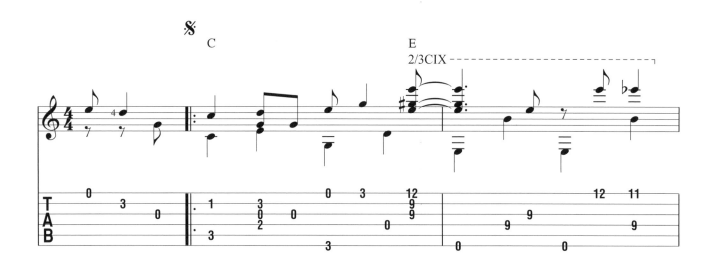

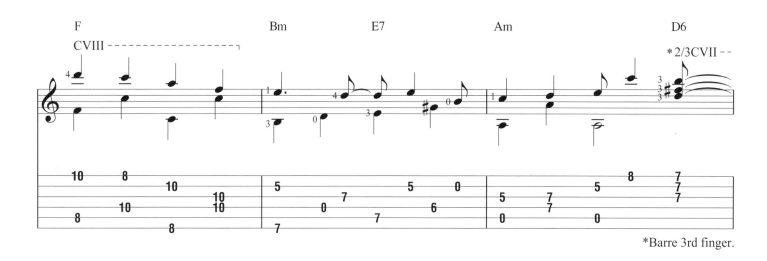

*Barre 3rd finger.

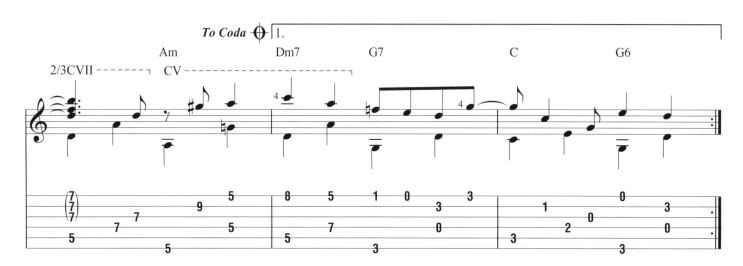

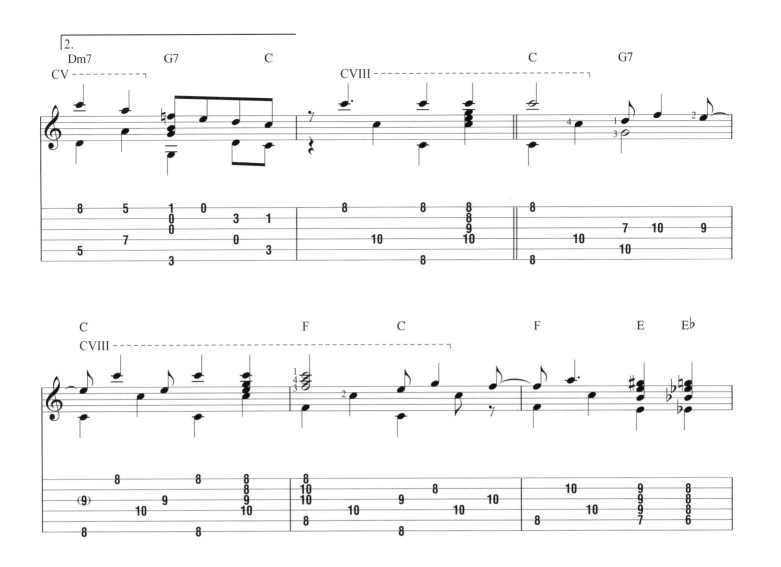

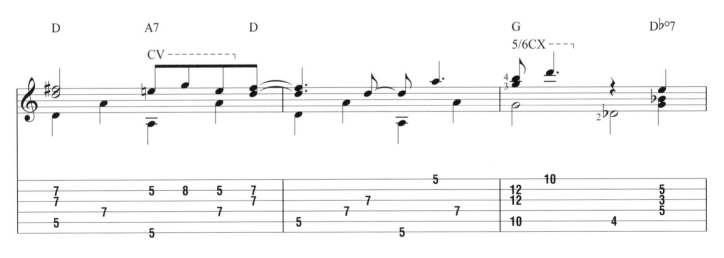

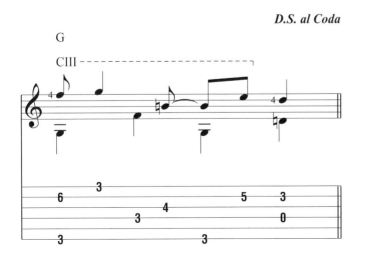

Some of These Days

Words and Music by Shelton Brooks

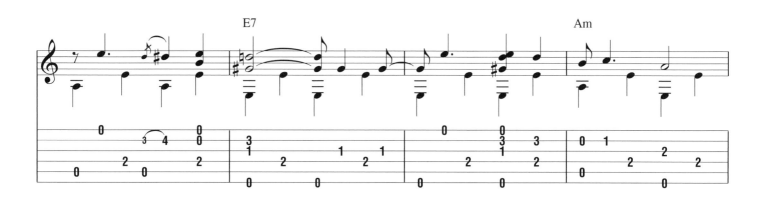

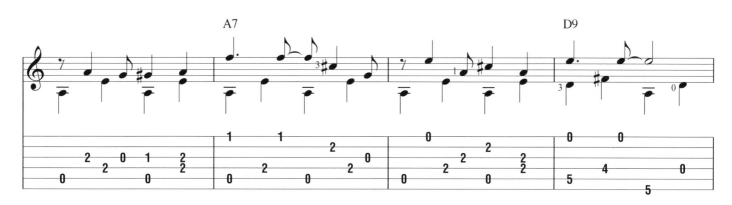

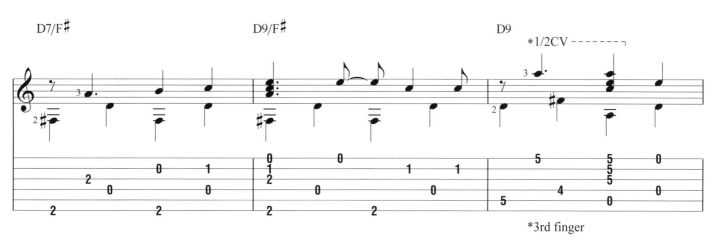

*3rd finger

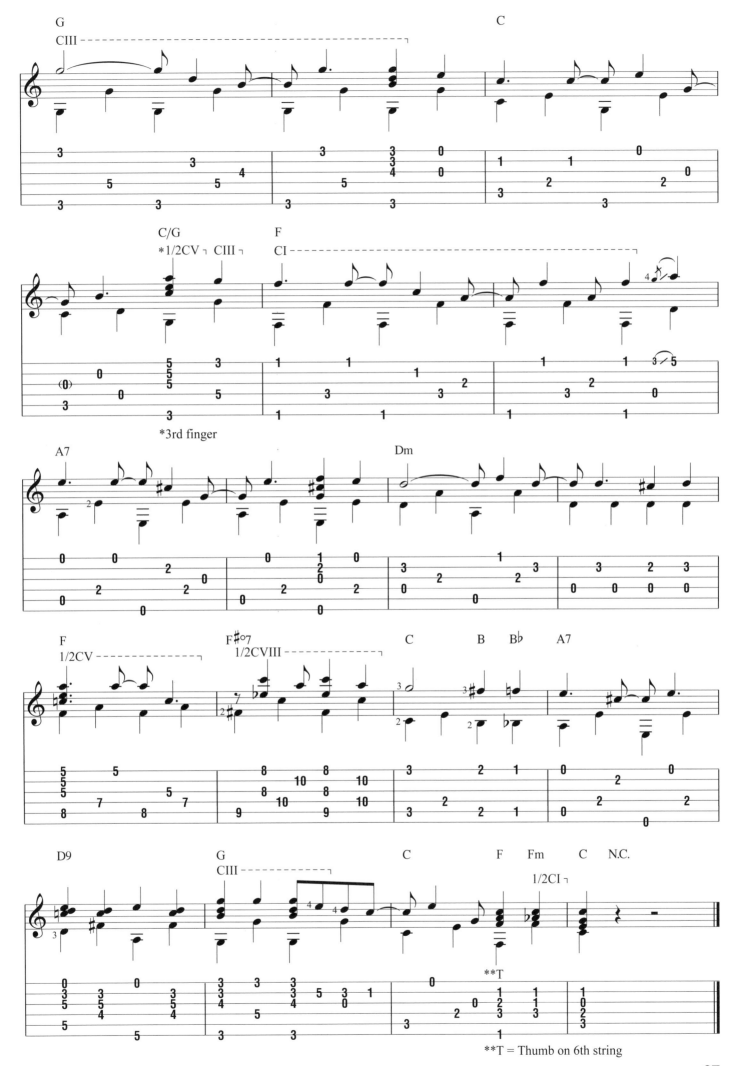

*3rd finger

**T = Thumb on 6th string

Stormy Weather
(Keeps Rainin' All the Time)

from COTTON CLUB PARADE OF 1933

Words by Ted Koehler
Music by Harold Arlen

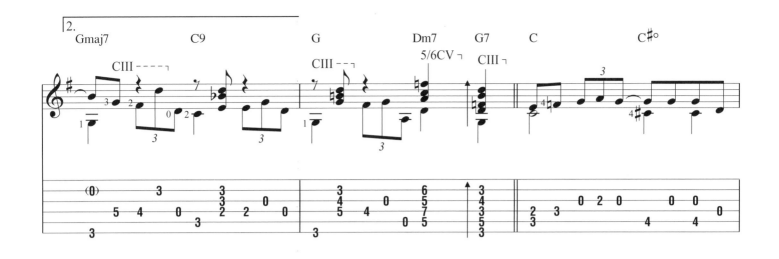

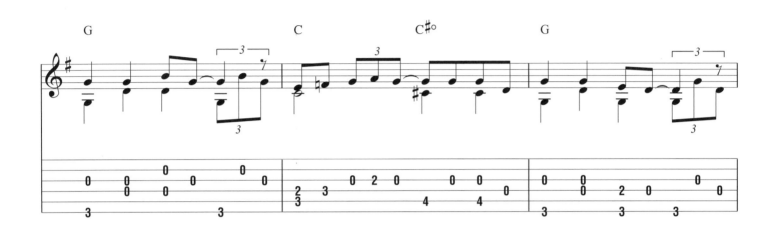

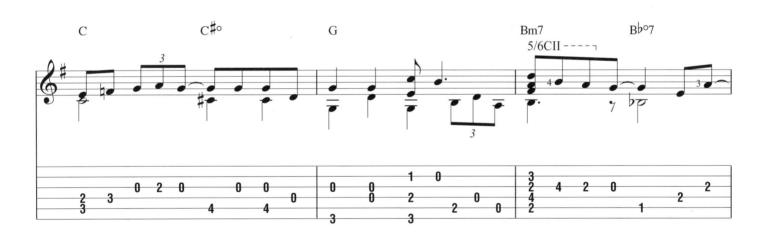

D.S. al Coda

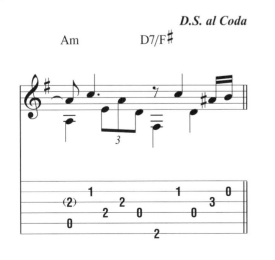

⊕ **Coda**

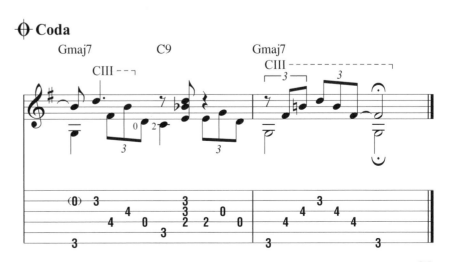

Sweet Georgia Brown

Words and Music by Ben Bernie, Maceo Pinkard and Kenneth Casey

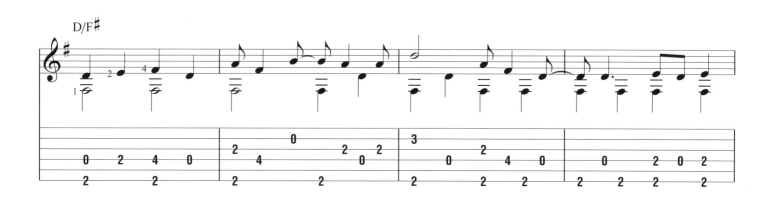

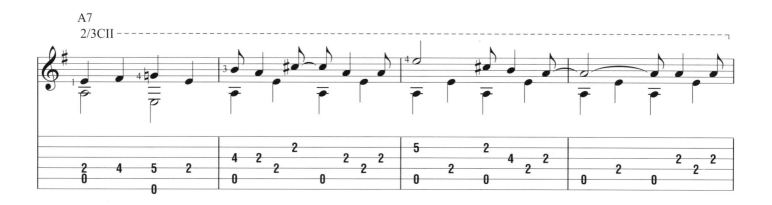

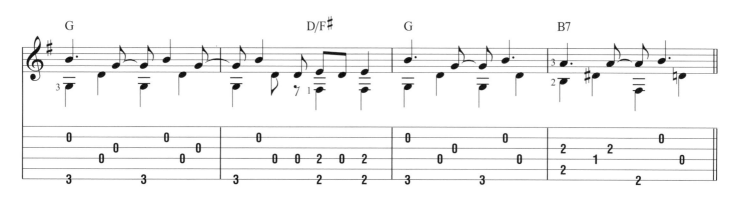

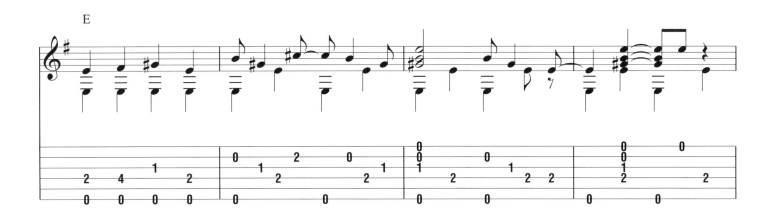

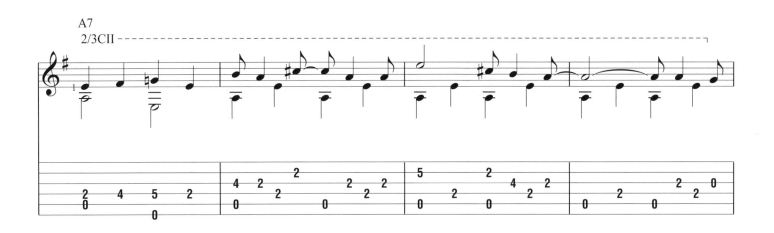

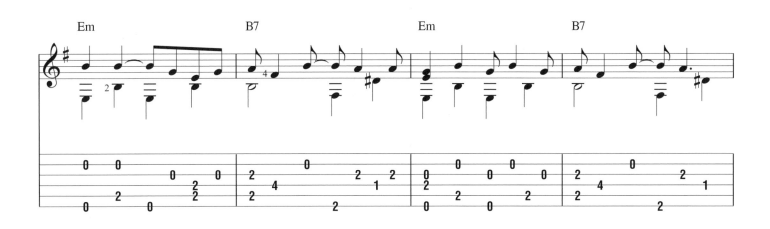

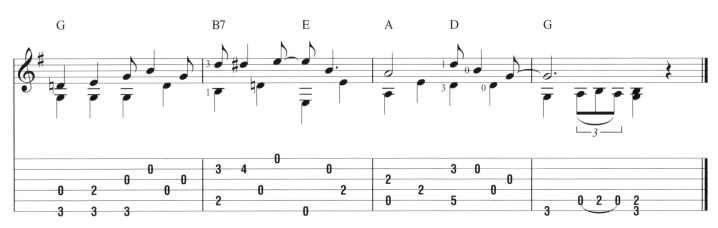

When It's Sleepytime Down South

Words and Music by Clarence Muse, Otis Rene and Leon Rene

*T = Thumb on 6th string

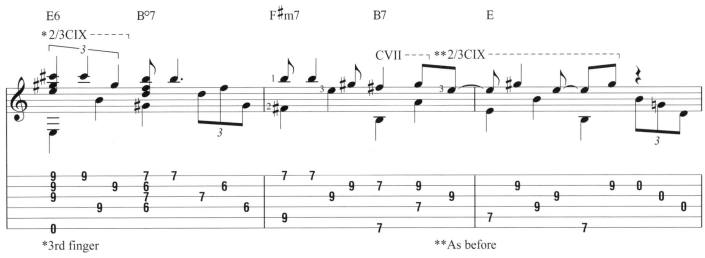

*3rd finger   **As before

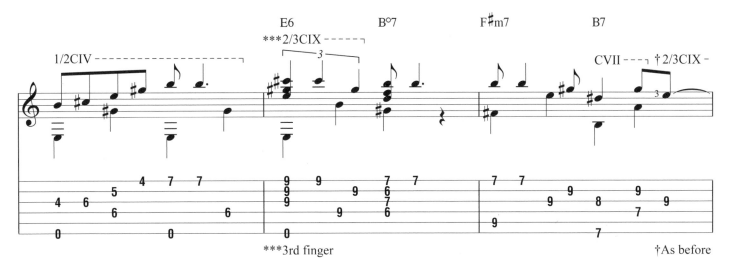

***3rd finger   †As before

D.S. al Coda   ⊕ **Coda**

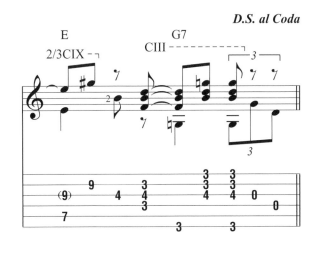

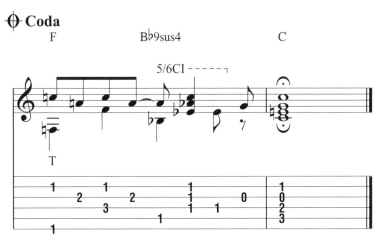

You Took Advantage of Me
from PRESENT ARMS
Words by Lorenz Hart
Music by Richard Rodgers

*T = Thumb on 6th string

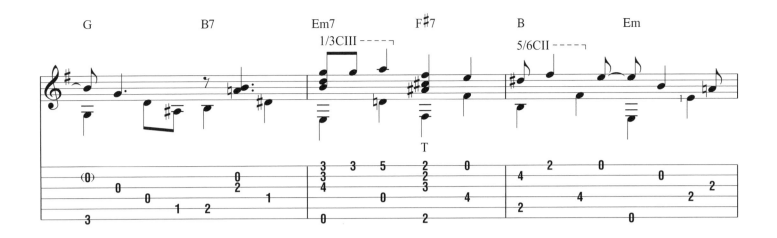

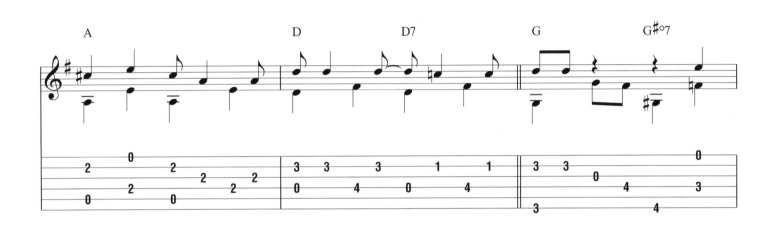

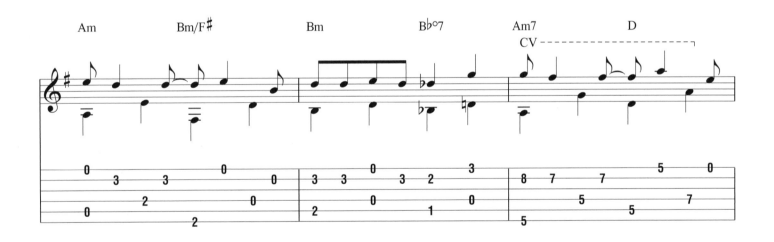

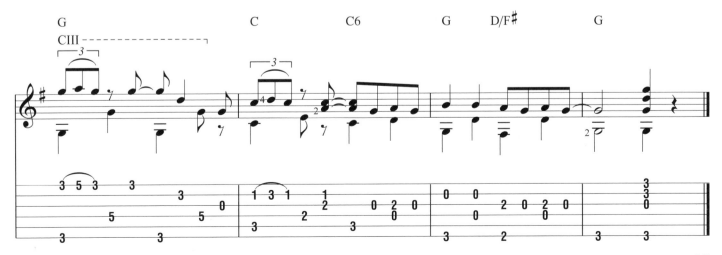

FINGERPICKING GUITAR BOOKS

Hone your fingerpicking skills with these great songbooks featuring solo guitar arrangements in standard notation and tablature. The arrangements in these books are carefully written for intermediate-level guitarists. Each song combines melody and harmony in one superb guitar fingerpicking arrangement. Each book also includes an introduction to basic fingerstyle guitar.

    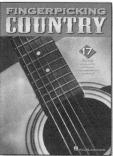 

Fingerpicking Acoustic
00699614 15 songs.......................$14.99

Fingerpicking Acoustic Classics
00160211 15 songs.......................$16.99

Fingerpicking Acoustic Hits
00160202 15 songs.......................$12.99

Fingerpicking Acoustic Rock
00699764 14 songs.......................$16.99

Fingerpicking Ballads
00699717 15 songs.......................$15.99

Fingerpicking Beatles
00699049 30 songs.......................$24.99

Fingerpicking Beethoven
00702390 15 pieces.....................$10.99

Fingerpicking Blues
00701277 15 songs $12.99

**Fingerpicking
Broadway Favorites**
00699843 15 songs.......................$9.99

Fingerpicking Broadway Hits
00699838 15 songs.......................$7.99

Fingerpicking Campfire
00275964 15 songs.......................$14.99

Fingerpicking Celtic Folk
00701148 15 songs.......................$12.99

Fingerpicking Children's Songs
00699712 15 songs.......................$9.99

Fingerpicking Christian
00701076 15 songs.......................$12.99

Fingerpicking Christmas
00699599 20 carols.....................$12.99

**Fingerpicking
Christmas Classics**
00701695 15 songs.......................$7.99

Fingerpicking Christmas Songs
00171333 15 songs.......................$10.99

Fingerpicking Classical
00699620 15 pieces.....................$10.99

Fingerpicking Country
00699687 17 songs.......................$12.99

Fingerpicking Disney
00699711 15 songs.......................$17.99

**Fingerpicking
Early Jazz Standards**
00276565 15 songs.......................$12.99

Fingerpicking Duke Ellington
00699845 15 songs.......................$9.99

Fingerpicking Enya
00701161 15 songs.......................$16.99

Fingerpicking Film Score Music
00160143 15 songs.......................$12.99

Fingerpicking Gospel
00701059 15 songs.......................$9.99

Fingerpicking Hit Songs
00160195 15 songs.......................$12.99

Fingerpicking Hymns
00699688 15 hymns......................$12.99

Fingerpicking Irish Songs
00701965 15 songs.......................$10.99

Fingerpicking Italian Songs
00159778 15 songs.......................$12.99

Fingerpicking Jazz Favorites
00699844 15 songs.......................$12.99

Fingerpicking Jazz Standards
00699840 15 songs.......................$12.99

Fingerpicking Elton John
00237495 15 songs.......................$15.99

Fingerpicking Latin Favorites
00699842 15 songs.......................$12.99

Fingerpicking Latin Standards
00699837 15 songs.......................$17.99

**Fingerpicking
Andrew Lloyd Webber**
00699839 14 songs.......................$16.99

Fingerpicking Love Songs
00699841 15 songs.......................$14.99

Fingerpicking Love Standards
00699836 15 songs $9.99

Fingerpicking Lullabyes
00701276 16 songs.......................$9.99

Fingerpicking Movie Music
00699919 15 songs.......................$14.99

Fingerpicking Mozart
00699794 15 pieces.....................$10.99

Fingerpicking Pop
00699615 15 songs.......................$14.99

Fingerpicking Popular Hits
00139079 14 songs.......................$12.99

Fingerpicking Praise
00699714 15 songs.......................$14.99

Fingerpicking Rock
00699716 15 songs.......................$14.99

Fingerpicking Standards
00699613 17 songs.......................$15.99

Fingerpicking Wedding
00699637 15 songs.......................$10.99

Fingerpicking Worship
00700554 15 songs.......................$14.99

**Fingerpicking Neil Young –
Greatest Hits**
00700134 16 songs.......................$17.99

Fingerpicking Yuletide
00699654 16 songs.......................$12.99

    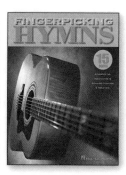 

JAZZ GUITAR CHORD MELODY SOLOS

This series features chord melody arrangements in standard notation and tablature of songs for intermediate guitarists.

> " Well-crafted arrangements that sound great and are still accessible to most players. "
>
> – *Guitar Edge* magazine

ALL-TIME STANDARDS

27 songs, including: All of Me • Bewitched • Come Fly with Me • A Fine Romance • Georgia on My Mind • How High the Moon • I'll Never Smile Again • I've Got You Under My Skin • It's De-Lovely • It's Only a Paper Moon • My Romance • Satin Doll • The Surrey with the Fringe on Top • Yesterdays • and more.
00699757 Solo Guitar $16.99

IRVING BERLIN

27 songs, including: Alexander's Ragtime Band • Always • Blue Skies • Cheek to Cheek • Easter Parade • Happy Holiday • Heat Wave • How Deep Is the Ocean • Puttin' On the Ritz • Remember • They Say It's Wonderful • What'll I Do? • White Christmas • and more.
00700637 Solo Guitar $14.99

CHRISTMAS CAROLS

26 songs, including: Auld Lang Syne • Away in a Manger • Deck the Hall • God Rest Ye Merry, Gentlemen • Good King Wenceslas • Here We Come A-Wassailing • It Came upon the Midnight Clear • Joy to the World • O Holy Night • O Little Town of Bethlehem • Silent Night • Toyland • We Three Kings of Orient Are • and more.
00701697 Solo Guitar $14.99

CHRISTMAS JAZZ

21 songs, including Auld Lang Syne • Baby, It's Cold Outside • Cool Yule • Have Yourself a Merry Little Christmas • I've Got My Love to Keep Me Warm • Mary, Did You Know? • Santa Baby • Sleigh Ride • White Christmas • Winter Wonderland • and more.
00171334 Solo Guitar $15.99

DISNEY SONGS

27 songs, including: Beauty and the Beast • Can You Feel the Love Tonight • Candle on the Water • Colors of the Wind • A Dream Is a Wish Your Heart Makes • Heigh-Ho • Some Day My Prince Will Come • Under the Sea • When You Wish upon a Star • A Whole New World (Aladdin's Theme) • Zip-A-Dee-Doo-Dah • and more.
00701902 Solo Guitar $14.99

DUKE ELLINGTON

25 songs, including: C-Jam Blues • Caravan • Do Nothin' Till You Hear from Me • Don't Get Around Much Anymore • I Got It Bad and That Ain't Good • I'm Just a Lucky So and So • In a Sentimental Mood • It Don't Mean a Thing (If It Ain't Got That Swing) • Mood Indigo • Perdido • Prelude to a Kiss • Satin Doll • and more.
00700636 Solo Guitar $14.99

FAVORITE STANDARDS

27 songs, including: All the Way • Autumn in New York • Blue Skies • Cheek to Cheek • Don't Get Around Much Anymore • How Deep Is the Ocean • I'll Be Seeing You • Isn't It Romantic? • It Could Happen to You • The Lady Is a Tramp • Moon River • Speak Low • Take the "A" Train • Willow Weep for Me • Witchcraft • and more.
00699756 Solo Guitar $17.99

JAZZ BALLADS

27 songs, including: Body and Soul • Darn That Dream • Easy to Love (You'd Be So Easy to Love) • Here's That Rainy Day • In a Sentimental Mood • Misty • My Foolish Heart • My Funny Valentine • The Nearness of You • Stella by Starlight • Time After Time • The Way You Look Tonight • When Sunny Gets Blue • and more.
00699755 Solo Guitar $16.99

LATIN STANDARDS

27 Latin favorites, including: Água De Beber (Water to Drink) • Desafinado • The Girl from Ipanema • How Insensitive (Insensatez) • Little Boat • Meditation • One Note Samba (Samba De Uma Nota So) • Poinciana • Quiet Nights of Quiet Stars • Samba De Orfeu • So Nice (Summer Samba) • Wave • and more.
00699754 Solo Guitar $16.99

Order online at **halleonard.com**

HAL•LEONARD®

IMPROVE YOUR IMPROV

AND OTHER JAZZ TECHNIQUES WITH BOOKS FROM HAL LEONARD

JAZZ GUITAR

HAL LEONARD GUITAR METHOD
by Jeff Schroedl

The Hal Leonard Jazz Guitar Method is your complete guide to learning jazz guitar. This book uses real jazz songs to teach the basics of accompanying and improvising jazz guitar in the style of Wes Montgomery, Joe Pass, Tal Farlow, Charlie Christian, Pat Martino, Barney Kessel, Jim Hall, and many others.
00695359 Book/Online Audio $22.99

AMAZING PHRASING

50 WAYS TO IMPROVE YOUR
IMPROVISATIONAL SKILLS • *by Tom Kolb*

This book explores all the main components necessary for crafting well-balanced rhythmic and melodic phrases. It also explains how these phrases are put together to form cohesive solos. Many styles are covered – rock, blues, jazz, fusion, country, Latin, funk and more – and all of the concepts are backed up with musical examples.
00695583 Book/Online Audio $22.99

BEST OF JAZZ GUITAR

by Wolf Marshall • Signature Licks

In this book/audio pack, Wolf Marshall provides a hands-on analysis of 10 of the most frequently played tunes in the jazz genre, as played by the leading guitarists of all time. Each selection includes technical analysis and performance notes, biographical sketches, and authentic matching audio with backing tracks.
00695586 Book/Online Audio $29.99

CHORD-MELODY PHRASES FOR GUITAR

by Ron Eschete • REH ProLessons Series

Expand your chord-melody chops with these outstanding jazz phrases! This book covers: chord substitutions, chromatic movements, contrary motion, pedal tones, inner-voice movements, reharmonization techniques, and much more. Includes standard notation and tab, and online audio.
00695628 Book/Online Audio $17.99

CHORDS FOR JAZZ GUITAR

THE COMPLETE GUIDE TO COMPING,
CHORD MELODY AND CHORD SOLOING • *by Charlton Johnson*

This book/audio pack will teach you how to play jazz chords all over the fretboard in a variety of styles and progressions. It covers: voicings, progressions, jazz chord theory, comping, chord melody, chord soloing, voice leading and many more topics. The audio offers 98 full-band demo tracks. No tablature.
00695706 Book/Online Audio $19.99

FRETBOARD ROADMAPS – JAZZ GUITAR

THE ESSENTIAL GUITAR PATTERNS
THAT ALL THE PROS KNOW AND USE • *by Fred Sokolow*

This book will get guitarists playing lead & rhythm anywhere on the fretboard, in any key! It teaches a variety of lead guitar styles using moveable patterns, double-note licks, sliding pentatonics and more, through easy-to-follow diagrams and instructions. The online audio includes 54 full-demo tracks.
00695354 Book/Online Audio $17.99

JAZZ IMPROVISATION FOR GUITAR

by Les Wise • REH ProLessons Series

This book/audio will allow you to make the transition from playing disjointed scales and arpeggios to playing melodic jazz solos that maintain continuity and interest for the listener. Topics covered include: tension and resolution, major scale, melodic minor scale, and harmonic minor scale patterns, common licks and substitution techniques, creating altered tension, and more! Features standard notation and tab, and online audio.
00695657 Book/Online Audio $19.99

JAZZ RHYTHM GUITAR

THE COMPLETE GUIDE
by Jack Grassel

This book/audio pack will help rhythm guitarists better understand: chord symbols and voicings, comping styles and patterns, equipment, accessories and set-up, the fingerboard, chord theory, and much more. The accompanying online audio includes 74 full-band tracks.
00695654 Book/Online Audio $24.99

JAZZ SOLOS FOR GUITAR

LEAD GUITAR IN THE STYLES OF TAL FARLOW,
BARNEY KESSEL, WES MONTGOMERY, JOE PASS, JOHNNY SMITH
by Les Wise

Examine the solo concepts of the masters with this book including phrase-by-phrase performance notes, tips on arpeggio substitution, scale substitution, tension and resolution, jazz-blues, chord soloing, and more. The audio includes full demonstration and rhythm-only tracks.
00695447 Book/Online Audio $19.99

100 JAZZ LESSONS

Guitar Lesson Goldmine Series
by John Heussenstamm and Paul Silbergleit

Featuring 100 individual modules covering a giant array of topics, each lesson includes detailed instruction with playing examples presented in standard notation and tablature. You'll also get extremely useful tips, scale diagrams, and more to reinforce your learning experience, plus audio featuring performance demos of all the examples in the book!
00696454 Book/Online Audio $24.99

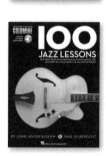

101 MUST-KNOW JAZZ LICKS

A QUICK, EASY REFERENCE GUIDE
FOR ALL GUITARISTS • *by Wolf Marshall*

Here are 101 definitive licks, plus demonstration audio, from every major jazz guitar style, neatly organized into easy-to-use categories. They're all here: swing and pre-bop, bebop, post-bop modern jazz, hard bop and cool jazz, modal jazz, soul jazz and postmodern jazz. Includes an introduction, tips, and a list of suggested recordings.
00695433 Book/Online Audio $19.99

SWING AND BIG BAND GUITAR

FOUR-TO-THE-BAR COMPING IN THE STYLE OF
FREDDIE GREEN • *by Charlton Johnson*

This unique package teaches the essentials of swing and big band styles, including chord voicings, inversions, substitutions; time and groove, reading charts, chord reduction, and expansion; sample songs, patterns, progressions, and exercises; chord reference library; and online audio with over 50 full-demo examples. Uses chord grids – no tablature.
00695147 Book/Online Audio $22.99

Prices, contents and availability subject to change without notice.